Colorado
Moments in Time

Photography & Text by Grant Collier

Collier Publishing
Lakewood, Colorado

CP

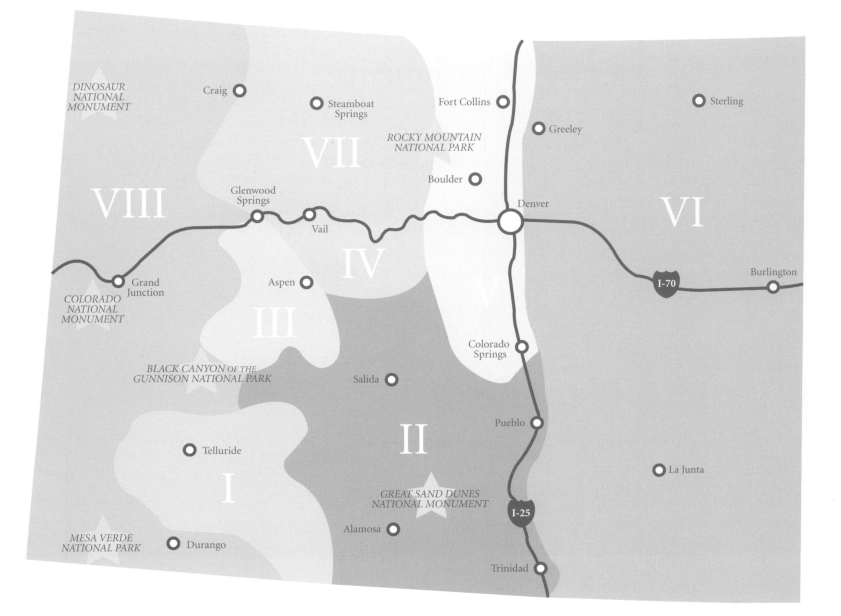

DINOSAUR
NATIONAL
MONUMENT

Craig

Steamboat
Springs

Fort Collins

Sterling

ROCKY MOUNTAIN
NATIONAL PARK

Greeley

VII

Boulder

VIII

Glenwood
Springs

Denver

VI

Vail

Grand
Junction

IV

Burlington

I-70

COLORADO
NATIONAL
MONUMENT

Aspen

III

V

BLACK CANYON OF THE
GUNNISON NATIONAL PARK

Salida

Colorado
Springs

Telluride

II

Pueblo

La Junta

GREAT SAND DUNES
NATIONAL MONUMENT

I

I-25

MESA VERDE
NATIONAL PARK

Durango

Alamosa

Trinidad

I.	San Juans
II.	South-Central Colorado
III.	Elk Mountains
IV.	Tenmile Range & Vicinity
V.	Front Range
VI.	Eastern Plains
VII.	Northern Rockies
VIII.	Western Slope

COLORADO *by* SECTION

Introduction

I SIT SUBMERGED UP TO MY WAIST in the cold waters of Maroon Lake, waiting for the sun to move into position. The sun always moves slowly at times like these. I recheck my tripod and camera, which I have carefully set up to capture both the reflected rays of light from the Maroon Bells and the refracted rays from the red rocks below the lake's surface.

Several people walk by, look at me with some perplexity, and continue on, amused by the sight of a foolish dilettante sitting in the middle of a freezing lake. One lady stops and, with obvious concern for both my health and my sanity, says, "That water must be awful cold. Perhaps you should come back in the morning when the lighting is best. I'm a bit of a shutterbug myself, but I wouldn't shoot in this lighting."

"Thanks," I say, wanting to tell her that I am attempting to get a more unique shot of the state's most photographed mountains. But there is no time. The sun is almost in position. That moment in time I've been waiting for is rapidly approaching.

I click the shutter release repeatedly to make sure I don't miss this shot. The sun soon vanishes behind the mountains (it moves quickly at times like these) and the moment is gone. I wade out of the lake, soaking wet and shivering, yet smiling and alive from the splendor of the moment. I wander slowly back along the path to my camp site, filled with a sense of wonder that is indispensable in life.

I would like to say that every minute I spend photographing in nature is as sublime as that ephemeral moment at the Maroon Bells. However, most of the time I spend in the field is fairly uneventful, sometimes even unpleasant. Hiking through rough terrain or driving for hours on end is not as romantic as some photographers may tell you. Ultimately, though, this makes the transcendent moments – when the lighting and scenery come together in a dazzling spectacle – that much more rewarding.

It is difficult for me to describe these moments, as language seems limited when faced with such a task. The Colorado landscape is simply too vast and intricate to fully depict in words. Theodore Roosevelt expressed this sentiment when he described a train ride he took to Cripple Creek in 1901 as "a trip that bankrupts the English language."

In many ways, a camera is not better suited to the task of portraying the majesty of Colorado's landscape than a pen. It can not reproduce the howling wind, the cool air, or the sheer enormity of the terrain. A photograph can, however, capture and preserve, if imperfectly, moments in time that would otherwise vanish forever. It allows for an artistic interpretation of the environment that can portray nuances of the light and the land. And it can provide testimony to the beauty of a natural landscape that could, in the coming years, be vastly altered by human activity.

Much of the environment has, of course, already been shaped by the hands of man. While Colorado is a land of vast open spaces and incredible scenery, it is also a land that has seen unprecedented development in recent years. It is a land that has been stressed by farming, ranching, mining, housing, and commercial development. While these activities are necessary for our survival and livelihood, it is imperative to find a balance between such endeavors and the preservation of open space.

It is my hope that the images in this book will lend to the argument that Colorado's remaining wild places need to be preserved; that open space is critical to our way of life; that our state's most important treasures lie not in our cities and towns, but in our unspoiled mountains, valleys, canyons, and grasslands.

I. San Juan Mountains

THE SAN JUAN MOUNTAINS in southwestern Colorado are awe-inspiring in their beauty. They harbor innumerable rivers, streams, lakes, and waterfalls, six wilderness areas, and a diverse population of wildlife. They contain more land above 10,000 feet than any other range in the continental U.S. and are home to thirteen 14,000 foot peaks. These mountains rise up very steeply and abruptly, giving them an air of majesty that is unrivaled in Colorado.

The first inhabitants of the San Juans are thought to have been the Ute Indians. These Native Americans infiltrated much of western Colorado following the departure of the Anasazi and Fremont Indians around 1300 A.D. Unlike their predecessors, who relied on farming, the Utes subsisted as hunters and gatherers. They stalked the large populations of deer, elk, antelope, rabbits, and beavers that were found throughout the region.

In addition to animal meat, the Utes also relied on berries that grew throughout the mountain valleys. It is believed that the Utes would leave the berries at the top of the trees untouched for the birds to eat. Likewise, the berries at the bottom of the trees were left for small animals to consume.

Like many other Native American tribes, the Ute Indians were a nomadic people. They lived at lower elevations during the winter and migrated to the San Juan Mountains during the warm summer months. Even during this relatively mild season, the living conditions in the rugged mountains were oftentimes harsh and unpredictable. Nevertheless the Utes revered the San Juans and called them "The Shining Mountains."

While living in these secluded mountains, the Utes seldom had to defend their land against competing tribes. They did, however, come into conflict with many of the Plains Indians when they migrated to lower elevations. These skirmishes became more pronounced after the arrival of the Spanish settlers in New Mexico in the 1600s. The Utes were the first tribe to acquire horses from the Spanish and they quickly became one of the most powerful and feared tribes in the region. They galloped out of the mountains to raid neighboring tribes, making off with supplies and capturing women and children.

Beginning in 1859, a large population of American miners and prospectors converged on Colorado and established settlements throughout the eastern Rockies. Few of these prospectors ventured into the western part of the state, and as a result the Ute Indians were able to avoid serious conflict with the early settlers for several years. This situation began to change in the 1870s when large amounts of silver and gold were discovered in the San Juans. Many prospectors descended on the area and tensions between the miners and the Utes began to escalate.

The Utes won a temporary victory in February of 1873 when the Department of the Interior ordered all miners to vacate the San Juan Mountains. This order was later suspended by the president, and soon afterwards the Utes were pressured into signing the Brunot Agreement, which reduced the size of their reservation by 3 million acres and opened the San Juans for mining.

As it turned out, the Brunot Treaty was only the beginning of the problems for the Utes. In 1879, members of the northern Utes revolted against Indian agent Nathaniel Meeker, killing him and eleven other men in what would become known as the Meeker Massacre. This incident created uproar throughout the state and led to the removal of the Northern Utes from Colorado in September of 1881. The Southern Utes were able to remain in Colorado due to the strong leadership exhibited by Chief Ouray. Today, these Native Americans inhabit the extreme southwest portion of the state.

While the Ute Indians no longer reside in the San Juan Mountains, they left a tremendous legacy in the region. Even today, in an era long removed from the pinnacle of Ute civilization, residents can learn from how this tribe lived. The Utes revered their homeland and respected the animals who shared the region with them. They realized that "The Shining Mountains" contained not only material resources to sustain their body, but spiritual elements to nourish their soul.

Wildflowers above Yankee Boy Basin.

Aspen bole fence below Mount Sneffels.

North Clear Creek Falls.

Lily pond along Molas Pass.

Last light on the San Juans.

Lizard Head Peak in winter.

Reflection of Lewis Mountain. La Plata Mountains.

Snowden Peak reflected in Little Molas Lake.

Cascades near Paradise Basin.

Mount Sneffels Range in winter.

Fall colors along the Dallas Divide.

Aspen contours on Miller Mesa.

Sneffels Creek. Yankee Boy Basin.

Falls below Clear Lake.

Indian paintbrush, sunflowers, and American bistort.

Aspen colors. Mount Sneffels Wilderness.

Red and orange hues of Anvil Mountain.

Parting colors. San Juan National Forest.

Preparing for winter. Uncompahgre National Forest.

Young sapling amidst imposing shadows.

Ice formations along Box Canyon.

II. South-Central Colorado

South-central Colorado is characterized by vast, sweeping valleys interspersed with spectacular mountain ranges. Much of this area is comprised of South Park and the San Luis Valley. Bordering these lowlands are immense mountain ranges, including the Collegiate Peaks to the west, the Sangre de Cristo Mountains to the east, and the Spanish Peaks to the southeast.

Zebulon Pike may have described this area best when, during his trek into the San Luis Valley in 1807, he wrote:

We ascended a high hill, which lay south of our camp, from whence we had a view of all the prairie and rivers to the north of us; it was at the same time one of the most sublime and beautiful inland prospects ever presented to the eyes of man … the great and lofty mountains, covered with eternal snows, seemed to surround the luxuriant vale, crowned with perennial flowers, like a terrestrial paradise shut out from the view of man.

During Pike's journey into the San Luis Valley, he came across one of Colorado's most unique natural features, known as the Great Sand Dunes. These ever-shifting mountains of sand were produced by the northeasterly winds that race across the San Luis Valley. These winds carry sand from throughout the region to the base of the Sangre de Cristo Mountains, where it accumulates into enormous mounds and knolls.

The Great Sand Dunes are surrounded by a number of small towns with such evocative and enchanting names as Monte Vista, Blanca, Rosita, and Querida. While these towns are now occupied by American citizens, the names are indicative of the legacy left by the early Spanish explorers in the region.

The Spanish explorers began infiltrating southern Colorado in the late 1600s. At the time, they were encroaching on land occupied by the Native Americans. Although the Spanish lived in peace with many of the tribes, the Comanche Indians strongly resisted their arrival. They frequently raided Taos and other New Mexico settlements and presented a constant threat to the early settlers.

In 1779, Governor Juan Bautista de Anza led hundreds of men into the San Luis Valley to confront the Comanche Indians. They failed to locate the tribe in this region and proceeded across the Front Range onto the eastern plains. Here they encountered the Comanches and soundly defeated the defiant tribe. After this devastating battle, the Comanche Indians signed a truce with the Spaniards and promised to end their raids on the New Mexico settlements.

Despite having sent expeditions throughout western America, the Spanish never did colonize the northern reaches of their territory. In 1800, much of this land, known as the Louisiana Territory, was claimed by Napoleon Bonaparte during the French Revolution. Three years later, Napoleon sold this territory to the United States for approximately $15 million.

At the time, the United States had little idea of what lay west of the Mississippi River, and it organized several expeditions to explore and map this new land. The first such expedition into southern Colorado was led by Zebulon Pike, who embarked on an arduous journey across the Great Plains in 1806. In November of that year, Pike and his men came within sight of the Rocky Mountains. Here they observed an impressive 14,000 foot mountain, which would later be named Pikes Peak. The party bypassed this mountain and headed up the Arkansas River, where they became disoriented and took a circuitous route that led them into the San Luis Valley. The group then crossed over the Rio Grande River and unknowingly entered Spanish territory. They were soon intercepted by Spanish scouts, who suspected the Americans of being spies. The Spanish escorted Pike and his men to Chihuahua, where they were questioned and finally released.

In contrast to the rather turbulent beginning experienced by early white explorers in the region, south-central Colorado today contains several quiet and peaceful communities. Unlike many cities in Colorado, which have seen rapid growth in recent years, these towns have experienced more steady and controlled growth. The pace of life remains relaxed and unhurried, and residents are not confronted with many of the urban problems, such as increased crime, overcrowding, and pollution.

Falls below Crestone Needle.

Double rainbow over South Park.

Reflection of Jenkins Mountain and Grizzly Peak.

Autumnal pond along the Gunnison River.

The Great Sand Dunes and Sangre de Cristo Mountains.

Southern sunflowers.

San Luis Lake during drought.

Approaching storm. Sangre de Cristo Range.

Evening light near Creede.

Rio Grande River near New Mexico.

Zapata Falls in winter.

Sun rays over the Collegiate Peaks.

Formations and shadows along the Great Sand Dunes.

Sand storm. Great Sand Dunes National Monument.

Wind-blown wheat near Saguache.

The Great Dikes of the Spanish Peaks.

Remnants of the Hayden Fire.

Volcanic rocks of Wheeler Geologic Area.

Patterns along rock wall. Wheeler Geologic Area.

III. Elk Mountains

The Elk Mountains lie deep in the heart of Colorado's Rocky Mountains. They encompass endless miles of enchanting, ethereal wilderness that has been largely untouched by man. Within this wilderness lie hidden lakes and ponds, pristine high-country streams, and a vast array of wildlife, from eagles and hawks to deer, coyotes, and foxes. The region also harbors two of the most famous icons in Colorado.

One of these icons is the Lost Horse Mill, located near the small town of Crystal. This structure was not actually a mill, but a power generating station. In the 19th century, it utilized energy from the adjacent waterfall to power an air compressor. The compressed air was then used to run machinery for the Sheep Mountain Mill.

Today, the generator has long since been shut down and the corroded, worn-down structure sits abandoned atop a small rock outcrop along the Crystal River. Unlike other ghost-buildings, the Lost Horse Mill has not been forgotten. It is one of the most scenic buildings in Colorado, and visitors come from throughout the world to view this remarkable structure.

While the Lost Horse Mill has gained significant fame, the Maroon Bells are probably the best known scenic attraction in the Elk Mountains. These twin 14,000 foot peaks rise dramatically above the glacially-carved valleys and basins of the Maroon Bells – Snowmass Wilderness Area. They are the most photographed mountains in Colorado and, like so many of Colorado's fourteeners, attract large numbers of rock climbers.

The Maroon Bells and the surrounding mountains gained their characteristic purple and red hues from sediment which was deposited during the erosion of the Ancestral Rockies over 200 million years ago. This sediment was thrust upwards during another period of mountain building, known as the Laramide Orogeny, beginning approximately 70 million years ago. This uplift, which resulted from massive tectonic forces, created the foundation for the Rocky Mountains that we see today.

While the Rocky Mountains were not formed by volcanic activity, as some originally thought, the state does have a very fiery past. Approximately 35 million years ago, enormous amounts of magma began to squeeze through cracks in the earth's surface, forming a chain of volcanoes from present-day Rocky Mountain National Park all the way to the San Juan Mountains. The volcanic activity was exceptionally violent in the West Elk Range, where eruptions rocked the area approximately 30 million years ago. These volcanoes buried the region with volcanic embers and ash and reeked havoc on the plant and animal populations in the area.

The Rockies were beset not only by fire, but by ice. Beginning approximately two million years ago, the earth was besieged by a series of ice ages that caused glaciers to periodically advance and retreat into Colorado's Rocky Mountains. As these glaciers gradually moved down the mountainsides, they carved out some of the more striking features of the Rockies, including steep valleys and basins, glacial moraines, and jagged mountain ranges. Evidence of glacial activity can be seen throughout the Elk Mountains and is especially prominent in the West Elks, where the relatively soft sediments were more easily carved out by glaciers.

The last series of glaciers retreated less than 20,000 years ago. Since that time, the climate has been relatively mild and has allowed for human settlements to emerge and grow throughout the state. It is possible that another ice age could engulf the planet in the geologically-near future, causing massive glaciers to again advance into Colorado's Rocky Mountains. However, given the recent impact that human activity has had on the global climate, it is difficult to predict climate changes more than one-hundred years in advance.

Whatever the future holds in store, it is important that we recognize the myriad of forces that have been at work over millions of years to produce the scenic grandeur that exists in the Elk Mountains today. This knowledge can help us in making decisions about how best to use the landscape that we are so fortunate to have inherited.

The Maroon Bells.

Wildflowers below Gothic Mountain and Mount Crested Butte.

Multi-colored aspen along McClure Pass.

Aspen and cow parsnips.

Reflection of Cinnamon Mountain.

Clearing storm over Lizard Lake.

Hays Creek Falls in winter.

Lost Horse Mill and the Crystal River.

Aspen leaves caught in an eddy.

Aspen colors along Marcelina Mountain.

Summer wildflowers. White River National Forest.

Maroon Bells reflected in Maroon Lake.

Fog along Mount Sopris.

Trees in the mist.

Frozen pond near Marble.

Winter patterns. Raggeds Wilderness.

Abandoned structure near the old Boston Mine.

Purple daisies along Webster Pass.

Blue Lake below Wheeler Mountain.

Peru Creek near its headwaters.

Last light on Red Cone.

High-country waters near Argentine Pass.

Vibrant sunset in the southern Gore Range.

Debris from rock-slide.

Autumn colors near Sylvan Lake.

Snow and ice patterns on Dillon Reservoir.

Winterscape along Fremont Pass.

Early fall colors.

Dramatic light over alpine pond.

Bristlecone pines near Windy Ridge.

Winter sun over Dillon Reservoir.

V. Front Range

While the Front Range is commonly thought to include cities such as Denver, Fort Collins, and Colorado Springs, it is geologically defined as the mountain range directly west of these communities. It is the largest of approximately twelve major mountain ranges in Colorado and is composed of smaller ranges, such as the Rampart Range, Indian Peaks, the Mummy Range, and the Tarryall and Kenosha Mountains. These ranges possess an enormous variety of scenery, including lakes, rivers, waterfalls, hot springs, glaciers, and caves. They also contain six 14,000 foot peaks, including Longs Peak, Mount Evans, and Pikes Peak, which dominate the skyline along the eastern plains.

At the base of the Front Range lie many impressive red rock formations in areas such as the Garden of the Gods, Roxborough State Park, Red Rocks Park, and the Boulder Flatirons. These formations had their beginnings some 280 million years ago, when the Ancestral Rocky Mountains – a precursor to today's Rocky Mountains – ruled the landscape. As the Ancestral Rockies eroded away, they left sediment known as the Fountain Formation, which gradually compacted into sandstone. When the modern Rocky Mountains began forming some 70 million years ago, this sandstone was uplifted and fractured. Over time, wind and water has eroded and sculpted the sandstone, thus forming the rock formations seen today.

Around the same time that these rock formations were taking shape, magma began to seep through cracks and openings that were formed as the Rocky Mountains were uplifted. This magma carried with it mineral-rich solutions, including gold and silver. Millions of years after these minerals were deposited they would drastically alter the course of human history along Colorado's Front Range.

In 1858, after hearing rumors that Cherokee Indians had discovered gold in present-day Colorado, the Russell party, led by brothers Oliver, Green, and Levi, came west in search of this elusive mineral. After several tiresome weeks, they finally discovered a small patch of gold near present-day Denver. As word of their discovery leaked out, the extent of their find became greatly exaggerated, and in the spring of 1859 approximately 100,000 enthusiastic prospectors set out for the Front Range of Colorado. Many of these prospectors were discouraged by what they found and quickly returned home. Others remained, determined to forge a living at the base of the rugged Rocky Mountains.

The aspirations of these early prospectors lay in finding substantial amounts of gold where only small amounts had previously been discovered. Their hopes were realized in January of 1859 when George Jackson discovered placer gold near present-day Idaho Springs. Soon afterwards, John Gregory made the first discovery of lode-gold near present-day Central City.

These discoveries helped secure the future of American settlement in Colorado. As word of the finds spread, a rush of prospectors headed to the north and south forks of Clear Creek. In short time, many new mining camps sprang up along the Front Range. Neighboring communities, such as Denver and Golden, also benefited, as they became supply towns for the mining communities.

While these early towns faced much adversity and struggled to survive, they helped shape the future of Colorado. Today, some of the mountain towns have become ghost towns, but others have been transformed into ski towns, gambling resorts, or tourist communities.

The towns lying east of these mountains communities, including Denver, Fort Collins, Boulder, Greeley and Colorado Springs, have seen the most growth and prosperity. While little gold or silver was discovered in this region, the cities have benefited from the milder weather conditions that prevail along the base of the Front Range. The growth of these communities has been especially rapid in recent times and many residents have become concerned that the area is growing too quickly and becoming overcrowded. This topic will likely garner much political debate in the coming years, and the solution that is ultimately agreed upon could dramatically alter the course of history in Colorado.

Flatirons in the fog.

Hallett Peak reflected in Dream Lake.

Fall River. Rocky Mountain National Park.

Boulder Falls in winter.

Rock formations at Red Rocks Park.

December sky.

Lightning strike on North Table Mountain.

Aspen reflection.

Aspen grove. Rocky Mountain National Park.

Autumn colors. Crown Hill Park Wildlife Refuge.

Driftwood patterns.

Summer in Garden of the Gods.

Spring bloom in Red Rocks Parks.

View from Rollins Pass.

Snow and ice patterns.

Cathedral Rock and South Gateway Rock. Garden of the Gods.

Nymph Lake reflection.

Columbine, Colorado's state flower.

Bristlecone pine at Mount Goliath Natural Area. Mount Evans.

Albino tree at Sherwin Lake.

VI. Eastern Plains

When one thinks of Colorado, majestic snow-packed peaks and enchanting mountain valleys tend to come to mind. However, nearly half of the state consists not of mountains and peaks, but of a vast, generally flat landscape that marks the western end of the Great Plains. While this area is oftentimes overlooked, it is nevertheless a land of striking beauty. It contains buttes, mesas, canyons, rivers, and endless miles of prairies that stretch as far as the eye can see.

The first humans to lay eyes on the eastern plains of Colorado were known as the Paleo-Indians. They arrived in Colorado approximately 12,000 years ago and are thought to be descendants of the northeastern Asian tribes who came to America via the Bering Strait some 20,000 years ago. The Paleo-Indians probably entered Colorado from the north, after passing through the area of present-day Wyoming. They are believed to have hunted big game, such as the mammoth and giant bison, that roamed the Great Plains during this time.

Succeeding the Paleo-Indians in eastern Colorado were the Archaic people, who appeared around 5000 B.C. Unlike their predecessors, these inhabitants relied on small game and the gathering of wild plants to procure food. This change was necessitated by the extinction of the giant bison and other large mammals following the end of the Ice Age.

Around 100 A.D., the Woodland culture emerged in the eastern plains. These Native Americans introduced pottery, houses, and farming to eastern Colorado. While these advancements represented a significant step in the development of Native American culture, the Woodland people continued to live much like their ancestors. They relied mostly on hunting and gathering and pursued the deer, bison, elk, and rabbits that inhabited the region.

In the late 1600s, Spanish explorers began penetrating the eastern plains of present-day Colorado. They were soon joined by French traders and explorers. The Native Americans, who already had to defend against competing tribes, were forced contend with these newcomers as well. Some tribes become allies with the French or the

Spanish, while others became bitter enemies of the intruders. This period was marked by shifting alliances and general unrest among the inhabitants.

In 1803, the United States purchased the Louisiana Territory from France and took possession of the eastern plains of Colorado. Initially, an uneasy peace existed between the Native Americans and the American explorers. However, in 1859, gold discoveries brought a flood of new prospectors across the overland trails in eastern Colorado. The Plains Indians became concerned that the prospectors were encroaching too rapidly upon their land, and in 1863 and 1864 raids by these tribes began to increase significantly.

The early American settlers became enraged by these attacks and called for action to ensure safe passage through the territory. Their demands were eventually met when, on November 29, 1864, over one-hundred Cheyenne and Arapahoe Indians, including many women and children, were killed in what would become known as the Sand Creek Massacre. This unfortunate incident marred Colorado's reputation for many years and led to the ultimate demise of the Plains Indians in Colorado.

Today, the Plains Indians have long departed from eastern Colorado and the landscape is dotted with small farming communities. Like the Native Americans before them, the farmers in these communities depend on Mother Nature for their livelihood. Water issues have been one of the top concerns for residents as long as anyone can remember. Some of these issues have been addressed by constructing reservoirs and tunnels to store water and divert it from western Colorado to the eastern plains. These projects have not alleviated all of the difficulties, as evidenced by the drought that has plagued Colorado in recent years. This drought has seriously affected the farmers in eastern Colorado, and if it continues for a prolonged period of time it could drastically affect the future of the plains.

Multi-colored vegetation near the Arkansas River.

West Butte at sunset. Pawnee National Grasslands.

Sunflower field near Johnstown.

Stately old trees in Otero County.

Autumn reflection. Cottonwood State Wildlife Area.

Wind-blown field near the Kansas border.

Natural grass along the Arickaree River.

Evening light near the Purgatoire River.

Hoodoo formations at the Paint Mines near Calhan.

Colorful rock formations at the Paint Mines.

Cactus bloom. Comanche National Grasslands.

Rock face in Vogel Canyon.

Isolated trees on the open plains.

Fall colors. Castlewood Canyon.

Union Slough Wildlife Refuge in northeast Colorado.

The bell-shaped East Butte. Pawnee National Grasslands.

Winter pasture.

Waves of snow.

VII. Northern Rockies

The northern Rockies of Colorado are the birth-place of some of the largest rivers in the western U.S., including the Colorado, North Platte, South Platte, and Yampa. These rivers begin as trickles of water high atop the snow-capped peaks of the Gore Range, the Park Range, the Front Range, and Rabbit Ears Range. As the water droplets move down the mountainsides, they collate into rivulets, which eventually merge into larger streams and rivers. The rivers spread out across the state and ultimately wind through vast regions of the western United States. Some roar through immense canyons such as the Grand Canyon and Desolation Canyon. Others meander slowly along the Great Plains in eastern Colorado and Nebraska. A few merge into even larger rivers, such as the Missouri and the Green, and they eventually distribute water to such distant lands as California and Louisiana.

The rivers and lakes in the northern Rockies of Colorado attracted many trappers and traders in the early 1800s, including such legendary men as Kit Carson, Jim Bridger, Louis Vasquez, and Jim Baker. These men came in search of valuable beaver pelts, which drew six to eight dollars apiece. While the mountain men initially thrived in Colorado and the western United States, the beaver supply gradually began to diminish as more and more trappers infiltrated the region. By the 1840s, most of these men were forced to abandon their livelihood. Many of the trappers returned east, while some became guides for government-funded expeditions in the West.

The first such expedition into northern Colorado was led by John Fremont during the second of his five historic missions to the western United States. Fremont, who was guided by the famed mountain man Kit Carson, traveled up the Cache La Poudre River in 1844 in an unsuccessful attempt to locate a passable route through the river canyon. The party then entered North Park, which Fremont described as follows:

The valley narrowed as we ascended, and presently degenerated into a gorge, through which the river passes as through a gate. We entered it, and found ourselves in the New Park – a beautiful circular valley of thirty miles diameter, walled all around with snowy mountains, rich with water, and with grass, fringed with pine on all mountain sides below the snow line, and a paradise to all grazing animals.

The next significant scientific exploration through northern Colorado took place in 1867, when Major John Wesley Powell led a private expedition to collect specimens of animals, plants, and minerals in the Rocky Mountains. The party first visited South Park and then headed north to explore the headwaters of the Colorado River.

Powell returned to northern Colorado the following year, during which time he and his men made the first known ascent of Longs Peak. Powell made some important scientific observations during these journeys, but he is better remembered today for his momentous 1869 voyage down the Green and Colorado Rivers.

Following Powell's expedition, F.V. Hayden visited northern Colorado as part of the Geological and Geographical Survey of the Territories under the Department of the Interior. Hayden was well-known for his reconnaissance of the Yellowstone area in 1871, which led to the creation of Yellowstone National Park. Hayden did some significant work in Colorado as well, and he developed some of the first scientific maps of the state.

Hayden's survey in Colorado came into conflict with another survey that was being conducted by Lieutenant George M. Wheeler for the War Department. This clash led to a congressional investigation to determine whether the surveys should be carried out by the Interior Department or the War Department. Ultimately, it was decided that there was enough work for both units, and each survey was told to proceed as planned.

Today, a number of the early expeditions into the northern Rockies of Colorado have been largely forgotten. Nevertheless, all of these missions played an integral part in shaping the future of the territory. When these parties embarked on their journeys, the area was wild, untamed, and almost entirely unknown. These expeditions shed light on the land and paved the way for the colonization and development of Colorado and the western United States.

Indian paintbrush.

Reflection in Trappers Lake.

Slater Creek and Long Mountain.

Early wooden pier near Kremmling.

Patterns of water and ice.

Ice formations along the Colorado River.

Beaver pond in Routt National Forest.

The Little Snake River near the Wyoming border.

Hahns Peak in late winter.

Aspen and spruce in Routt National Forest.

Falls along the Elk River.

Red and black banded walls along the Cache la Poudre River.

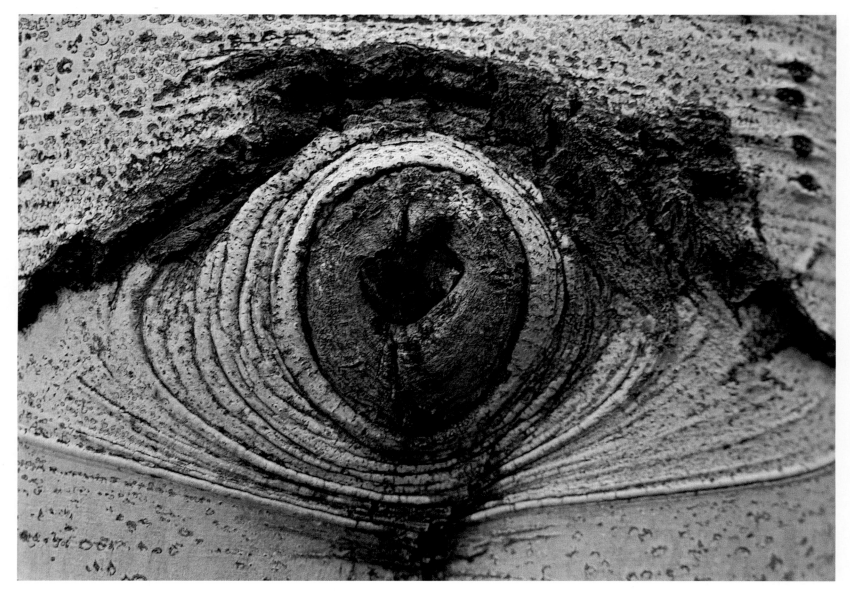

Aspen eye.

Twin trees north of Steamboat Springs.

Fall colors near Mount Zirkel Wilderness.

Aspen shadows in the Indian Peaks Wilderness.

Falls above Hanging Lake.

Clear waters of Piney River.

Charred trees from a forest fire.

Patterns along Morgan Creek.

VIII. Western Slope

In sharp contrast to the mountains of Colorado, the Western Slope is a stark desert landscape containing a labyrinth of plateaus, canyons, buttes, mesas, spires, arches, and rivers. Given the scenic wonders in the Rocky Mountains and Utah's red-rock wilderness, this landscape is oftentimes ignored by travelers. Nevertheless, it is one of the most spectacular places on the planet. From the Anasazi ruins in Mesa Verde National Park to the enormous canyons in Dinosaur National Monument, Colorado's Western Slope is a land of amazing beauty.

Mesa Verde National Park was established in 1906, making it the first national park to be created in Colorado and the tenth national park in the United States. It was established to preserve and protect the villages and artifacts constructed by the Anasazi Indians over seven hundred years ago.

The Anasazis were one of the most remarkable tribes ever to inhabit Colorado. They were the first culture to introduce farming to the region, and they constructed reservoirs to help cultivate their crops. They also built impressive villages atop the mesas in the Four Corners area. Around 1100 A.D., the Anasazi Indians moved their villages to protective rock overhangs along canyon walls. Less than two-hundred years later, for reasons not entirely known, the Anasazis vanished from Colorado.

While Mesa Verde National Park contains man-made attractions, most of the scenic wonders along the Western Slope have natural origins. These marvels include the Dolores Canyon, Black Canyon of the Gunnison, and the canyons of Dinosaur National Monument. Each of these canyons was formed as the surrounding land was uplifted, thus forcing the Dolores, Gunnison, Yampa, and Green rivers to carve out enormous canyons along the Western Slope.

While the canyons were all formed in a similar manner, each of them is geologically unique. The Black Canyon of the Gunnison contains steep canyon walls exceeding 2,000 feet in height which drop precipitously down to the river. These walls contain some of the oldest exposed rock in the world.

Unlike the Black Canyon, the Dolores River Canyon in southwestern Colorado has a moderate slope, devoid of sheer rock walls. It is, however, no less impressive than the Black Canyon. The canyon is over 2,000 feet deep and its contours are reminiscent of the Grand Canyon. The walls of Dolores Canyon are composed of a variety of different rock formations which reveal the rich and diverse geologic history of the area.

The long, winding canyons in Dinosaur National Monument were carved out by the Yampa and Green Rivers, which merge within the park. These canyons lie near the northeast boundary of the Colorado Plateau and are composed of several different rock formations which harbor numerous fossils, including those of the dinosaurs.

While the canyons along the Western Slope were formed by the steady and continual surges of rivers, the formations in Colorado National Monument were created by more subtle processes. Rain storms and melting snow have carried away much sediment, contributing to erosion in the area. The rock has been further weakened as water seeped into cracks, froze, and expanded. Other forces, such as wind and even plant growth, have put the finishing touches on the erosion of rock formations in Colorado National Monument.

These rocks have not eroded to a level surface because they are capped by sandstone of the Kayenta Formation. This sandstone is harder and more resistant to erosion than the Wingate Sandstone that lies beneath it. As the surrounding Wingate Sandstone has eroded away, some remnants of the Kayenta Formation have remained intact, allowing for the formation of the enormous buttes and spires.

The forces that have carved out the impressive scenery along the Western Slope are still at work today. Water continues to gradually, but persistently break down rocks and carry the sediment downstream. It will continue to do so far into the future. In the process, impressive new rock formations and ever deeper canyons will be created, all of which will likely be marveled at by future generations.

Cliff Palace. Mesa Verde National Park.

Anasazi Ruins in Mesa Verde National Park.

Remnants of Mesa Verde forest fire.

Last light. Black Canyon of the Gunnison National Park.

Cloud reflections. Dolores River Canyon.

Rock formations along the Dolores River.

Dolores Canyon Overlook near Uravan.

Reflection in John Brown Canyon.

Grand View Spire. Colorado National Monument.

Piñon pine and spire. Colorado National Monument.

Hole-in-the-Bridge Arch. Rattlesnake Canyon.

Akiti Arch (also known as East Rim Arch). Rattlesnake Canyon.

Aspen forms along Grand Mesa.

Evening reflection on Grand Mesa.

Rifle Falls.

Morning light in Dinosaur National Monument.

Reflection of Steamboat Rock. Dinosaur National Monumnet.

Gates of Lodore. Dinosaur National Monument.

Further Reading

Chronic, Halka & Williams, Felicie. *Roadside Geology of Colorado*. Missoula, Montana: Mountain Press Publishing Company, 2002.

Collier, Grant. *Colorado: Yesterday & Today*. Montrose, Colorado: Western Reflections Publishing Company, 2001.

Crum, Sally. *People of the Red Earth*. Santa Fe, New Mexico: Ancient City Press, 1996.

Ubbelohde, Carl; Benson, Maxine; Smith, Duane A. *A Colorado History*. Boulder, Colorado: Pruett Publishing Company, 2001.

Acknowledgements

Many thanks to Catamount Mayhugh & Dax Oliver.